The Checker Playing Hound Dog

Tall Tales from a Southwestern Storyteller
Joe Hayes

For Lanie —
there
Enjoy
whoppers!

Joe Hayes
1995

illustrations by Lucy Jelinek

a **Mariposa** Book

Published by
Mariposa Publishing
922 Baca Street
Santa Fe, New Mexico 87501
(505) 988-5582

THIRD PRINTING 1990
FIRST PRINTING 1986

Selections from "The Day It Snowed Tortillas,"
"Coyote &," "The Checker Playing Hound Dog" and
"A Heart Full of Turquoise" by Joe Hayes available
on cassette tapes from
Trails West Publishing, P.O. Box 8619,
Santa Fe, New Mexico 87504-8619.

ISBN 0-933553-04-8

**To children
of all ages**

ALSO FROM MARIPOSA PUBLISHING

Children's Literature
By Joe Hayes

The Day It Snowed Tortillas
Tales from Spanish New Mexico

Coyote &
Native American Folk Tales

A Heart Full of Turquoise
Pueblo Indian Tales

By Gerald Hausman

Turtle Dream
Ghost Dance

Adult Literature

By Robert Mayer

Sweet Salt, A Novel

TABLE OF CONTENTS

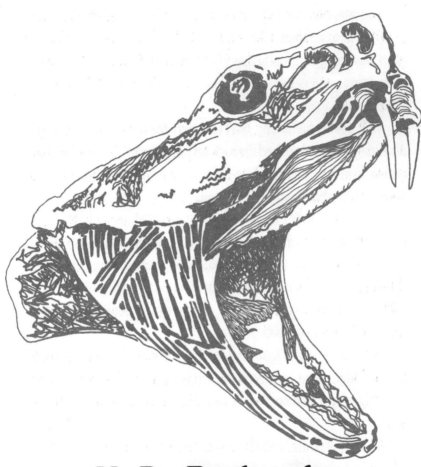

My Pet Rattlesnake

I do believe the most misunderstood animal in the West is the rattlesnake. Most people are just terrified of rattlesnakes, when the truth is that they are the most kind, affectionate and warm-hearted of all snakes. Of course, I wouldn't know that either if it hadn't been for an experience I had when I was a boy.

7

You see, one day I was hiking around in the desert and I happened to hear a rattlesnake rattling. So I followed the sound to see what was going on. I found that a big rock had slid down off the bank of an arroyo and pinned the rattlesnake to the ground. He was rattling for help.

Well, I don't know why, but I felt sorry for that rattlesnake. I got me a long stick and pushed the rock off him. The rattlesnake lay there gazing up at me, and I could see from the look in his eye how much he appreciated what I had done for him.

I said, "Oh, that's all right. I don't mind helping you. Now you just go your way, and I'll go mine." And I turned and walked away.

I had gone about ten steps, when I happened to look behind me. Durned if the rattlesnake wasn't following me! I said, "No! You can't follow me. I have to go home. Now, you just go on your way." I patted him on the head, and walked away.

But the snake kept following me. I would speed up, and he would too. I'd dodge around a bend in the arroyo and then run to get ahead, but he'd always catch up. That rattlesnake followed me the whole way home!

When I got home I called my dad. "Hey, Dad," I said. "Can I keep this snake for a pet?"

My dad hollered, "What! Keep a rattlesnake for a pet?"

"But, Dad," I said, "What can I do? He followed me home."

My dad kind of scratched his chin. "Well . . . if he followed you home, you can keep him for a while. We'll see how it works out."

So I kept the rattlesnake for a pet. And, you know, he made a very good pet. He would tag along with me everywhere I went. Every night he slept right at the foot of my bed. In the morning I'd wake up and wiggle my toes and he'd nip at them real playfully.

Of course, he didn't use his fangs when he bit my toes. In fact, the only thing he did use his fangs for was to scratch on the screen door when he wanted to come inside. But that did cause a problem. You see, his fangs had a little bit of poison on them, and the poison would soak into the wood and make it swell up. The door was always hard to open. That kind of made my dad mad. He'd get his plane and shave off the edge of the door, but then it would swell up some more and start to stick again.

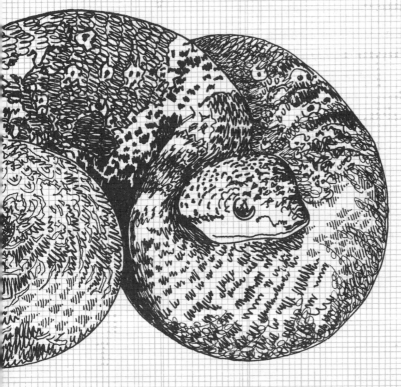

Then one day my dad looked at the screen door and said, "This door is getting awfully weather-beaten. I'd better paint it today." And he got a can of white paint and painted up the screen door.

But the paint had turpentine in it. And the turpentine drew the poison out of the wood. The edge of the screen door started shrinking back down again and it ended up about a half an inch wide!

My dad was pretty mad. And besides, the neighbors were complaining about my snake. They said he was going to bite someone. We knew he would never do that, but my dad told me the time had come for me to get rid of my pet. "Take your snake back out in the desert and leave him there," he told me.

So I took my snake for a walk in the desert. We went about two miles. Then I sat down under a big mesquite tree. My snake coiled up beside me and went to sleep.

As soon as he fell asleep, I jumped up and ran home. When I got home, you know what I saw? My rattlesnake! He was waiting for me by the door. He must have known some shortcut through the desert and he got home before I did.

My dad said, "We have to get rid of that snake!" So we put him in the trunk of the car and drove about thirty-five miles out into the desert and left him there.

I was so sad as we drove home. It was all I could do to keep from crying. That evening I had no appetite for supper. I couldn't sleep a wink that night.

The next morning I was sitting at the table eating a bowl of cereal—it had no flavor because I was feeling so sad—when I heard a noise over by the door. My heart just leaped up! I ran to the door, and there was my snake scratching to come inside. He had traveled all night long to get back home.

When my dad saw that, he said, "If that snake is going to travel thirty-five miles to live here with us, we're going to keep him. I don't care what the neighbors say!"

And that turned out to be the smartest decision he ever made in his life. I'll tell you why. Only about three weeks later, I woke up in the middle of the night and I heard my rattlesnake rattling. So I got my dad out of bed. He took his flashlight and went looking around the house. And I will be sixteen kinds of liar if a burglar hadn't broken into our house that night. And my rattlesnake had wrapped himself around the burglar's neck and had his tail hanging out the window—rattling for the police!

Isn't that the best watch rattlesnake you ever heard of in your life? I'm sure it is. And I would have that snake to this day—except that crazy fool animal developed a bad habit. He started chasing cars.

I tried and tried to break him of the habit because I knew it was just a matter of time until he'd get hit by a car. Then one day it happened. I got home from school and my snake didn't meet me at the gate. I ran around looking for him. I went out to the street, and sure enough, he had been run over. He was dead and just lying there on the pavement. Just like I've been lying to you on the pages you just read.

A Bucketful of Dust

I remember one time when I was sitting on the front porch of a ranch house talking to a friend of mine. We kind of gazed out across the prairie as we talked, and I'll tell you, that country was so flat we could see the bottom of a forty-foot well that was a good two miles away from where we sat. Well, things around there looked kind of dull and uninteresting to me, but my friend told me he never left that ranch, year in and year out.

I asked him, "Don't you ever get tired of this place? Don't you want to get out and see some new country?"

He laughed, "Oh, I get to see plenty of country. I can sit right here on this porch any day in the spring and just watch the country blow by."

I asked him to explain, and found out he was talking about dust storms. He said he had seen the dust so thick the buzzards all wore goggles. And they flew backwards to keep from choking on the flying sand.

Just then I noticed a puffy little cloud above the western horizon. I said maybe it would rain that day. Then he really laughed. "Rain?" he said. "Why it hasn't rained around here since Noah's flood. And even then it was hardly enough to wash the dirt off the mesquite leaves."

Sure enough, the next time I looked up the cloud was gone—just disappeared. I couldn't imagine living in such a place. "Don't you wish it would rain around here just once?" I asked.

"Oh, no, not really," he told me. "I spent a year in California when I was in the army as a young man. I saw it rain plenty." But then he looked at his old dad sitting in his rocking chair at the other end of the porch. "But, you know," my friend said, "sometimes I do wish it would rain a little for old Dad. He's eighty years old and he has never seen it rain. It might be nice for him to have that experience just once before he goes."

Well, the conversation moved on to other things and finally I had to leave. I never thought much more about it.

Then I got a letter from my friend about six months later, and he told me he had got his wish. His old dad was walking from the corral to the house one day and a tiny cloud came sailing along and dropped about a thimbleful of rain on his bald head.

And, do you know, that old man was so shocked at feeling water fall from the sky for the first time in his eighty years, he fainted out cold.

The rancher had to run quick and get a bucketful of dust and throw it in his face to wake him up!

Flying Fish

The mountains around here are famous for two things—bad weather and good fishing. In summer the thunderheads build up over these peaks till you'd think they could reach the moon. And when they let loose with a downpour, the trees and rocks have to hang on for dear life to keep from being washed away. Those storms keep all the streams full and roaring, and that's what makes the fishing so good.

I remember one summer day when I set out with my fishing pole and figured I'd try my luck in a little stream that ran a few miles from my home. There were tall white thunder clouds over in the west when I left home, and by the time I got close to my fishing stream, they were throwing mean looks at me from straight overhead.

Then, without so much as a warning drizzle, they opened up—whoosh! Luckily there was a hollow log nearby, and I dropped everything and dived into it for shelter. I could hear the rain beating against the log, and I felt it sort of heave and roll under me. But it was dark in there, so I didn't know what was going on. Then the rain stopped just as suddenly as it had started.

I lay inside the log for a while, listening to the slow dripping from the branches all around. Then I started backing myself out. But when my legs were clear of the end of the log, there wasn't anything to put them onto. They were kicking around in thin air. I backed up till I could grab the edge of the log with my hands and pushed the rest of me out into daylight.

What do you know! I was hanging in mid-air about thirty feet above the ground. That hollow log had floated right up into the rain and then when the storm had stopped it had settled into the top branches of a fir tree.

Well, I shinnied down the tree in no time, but my fishing pole and tackle were nowhere to be seen. It looked like I'd just have to forget about any fish for dinner. I turned and started home, when all of a sudden—*wham!*—something hit the ground in front of me with a sound like a board hitting a wet blanket.

I looked down at my feet and saw the biggest old granddaddy trout I had ever laid eyes on. It didn't take me long to figure out what had happened. That old trout had thought the rain storm was just another steep mountain stream and had swum right up it. Of course, when the rain stopped, down he came a-tumbling.

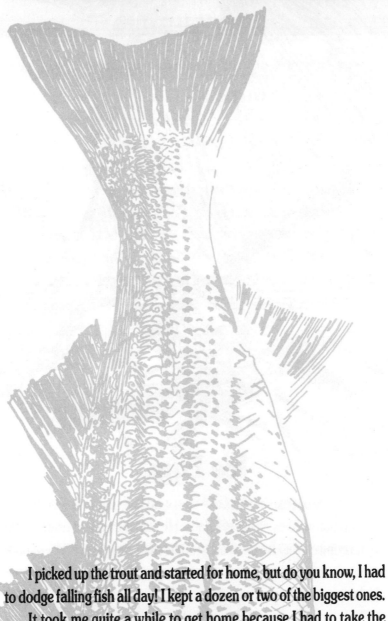

I picked up the trout and started for home, but do you know, I had to dodge falling fish all day! I kept a dozen or two of the biggest ones.

It took me quite a while to get home because I had to take the long way around so that I wouldn't run into the game warden. I had collected more than the legal limit of fish, and he probably wouldn't have believed my story—any more than you do!

Ice Eggs

A couple of years ago I met a man who had homesteaded out on the high plains back in the old days. He told me he had tried a little dry farming on that homestead. And he had some livestock—a milk cow and an old plow horse, maybe a goat or two. And he raised chickens.

Now, you may know about chickens. A hen will often make her nest in some dark corner or high and hard-to-get-at place because she doesn't want the farmer to find her eggs. She wants to hatch them out and have some babies.

Well, this man had one hen in his flock who was better than the rest at finding a secret spot to make her nest. But no matter how hard it was to find her eggs, the homesteader would make the effort, because that hen laid the biggest eggs of any hen on the farm. In fact, her eggs were so big, it only took eight of them to make a dozen!

But I think if my friend had known how badly the hen wanted to hatch out some eggs and be a mother, he would have let her nest alone. He didn't realize it, though, until one day when a terrible hail storm hit his farm.

Big balls of ice came battering down from the sky, knocking holes in the roofs of his buildings and beating the crops into the ground. When the worst of it was over, the homesteader went outside to see what the damage was. He walked over to the chicken coop, and there in the yard he saw a little pile of straw with six or eight big hail stones lying on it. They were just about the size of hen's eggs. In fact, it looked for all the world like a nest with a half dozen or so eggs in it.

And just about the same time the farmer saw the pile of straw, that silly old hen that wanted to be a mother so badly spied it too. She ran over and settled herself on top of the hail stones, clucking away as contented as you please. She thought she finally had some eggs to hatch.

The homesteader chuckled to himself. "That crazy old bird," he said. "She thinks she can hatch out those hail stones." He walked off shaking his head.

But that hen had made up her mind, and she was going to see the job through to the finish. Day after day the farmer saw her there, sitting on those balls of ice. He laughed and laughed at her, but I think the hen must have had the last laugh.

One morning the man went out to feed his chickens and there was that hen, strutting up and down the yard as proud as a preacher's momma—with a whole string of little penguins tagging along behind her. Yeah! She had hatched out those ice eggs.

My Pet Catfish

To be perfectly honest with you, I didn't really have any good place to fish when I was a boy—just little ponds here and there on the farms outside our town. But sometimes I did have pretty good luck in those ponds.

One time I couldn't believe the luck I was having! I would put a worm on my hook and drop it in the water, and bam! I'd have a fish. I would reel it in, toss it up on the bank, put a new worm on the hook and—*bam*—another fish—one right after the other.

I caught one old catfish and some blue gills and a couple of little sunfish. Then it got late and I had to go home. So I went around gathering up the fish I had caught. Of course they were all dead from lying out on bank. Except for the catfish. When I picked him up, he started flopping around in my hand.

Now, that sort of surprised me. The catfish had been one of the first fish I'd caught. So I went back over by the pond and found an old can. I filled it with water and dropped the catfish in. He started jumping around as frisky and perky as if he'd never been out of water at all!

Well, I started for home. And as I walked along I began to get curious about that catfish. I began to wonder just how long that crazy

24

fish could stay out of the water. And by the time I got home, I had decided to perform an experiment.

I left the catfish out in the yard all night long. In the morning I dropped him into a bucket of water. He revived in no time. So I left him out in the yard for a whole day—for twenty-four hours! I dropped him into the water and he came right around. I started making the time longer and longer that he was out of the water, and do you know, it only took me about three weeks to get that catfish trained so that he never had to go back into the water.

And he turned into a great little pet! He would flop along on the ground and follow me around all day long. He was easy to take care of. All I had to do was give him a worm every day or two. My mom liked him because he didn't make a mess in the back yard or scratch up the doors the way dogs always do.

He was just a great companion for me all summer long. But then the end of summer vacation came and I had to go back to school. The first day of school I started down the street for the bus stop and I got about half-way there when I happened to look behind me. Dang! My catfish was following me to the school bus!

I had to turn around and take him back home. I put him inside the yard and scolded him. "Stay!" I said and wagged my finger at him. "You stay! Don't follow me. Stay!"

I turned and ran back to the bus stop. But I was too late. I missed the bus. I was late for school the first day, and the teacher was mad at me before the year even got started. I think she stayed mad at me that whole year because I sure did get into a lot of trouble that year.

Anyway, school had been going on for about a month when I made a new friend. A new kid had moved to town and he was going to meet me at my house after school. But the teacher made me stay late and I didn't get home until about an hour after I expected to.

When I got home, my friend was waiting for me, but I didn't see my catfish anywhere. And he always came flopping out to greet me when I got home from school. I asked my friend, "Did you see a little fish around anywhere when you got here?"

"Oh, yeah," he said. "I saw him. He was flopping around on the ground, just going crazy. I felt sorry for him. I threw him in that bucket of water over there."

I screamed, "You did what?" I ran over to the bucket as fast as I could, but I was too late. My little fish had already drowned.

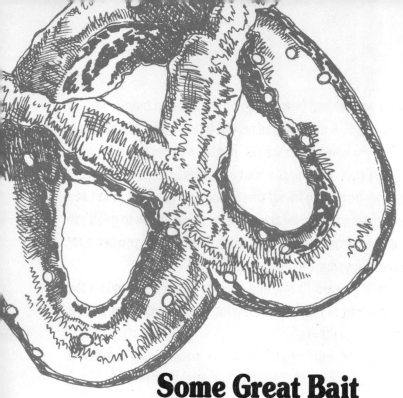

Some Great Bait

I can't think of a better way to spend a day than sitting on the bank of some favorite fishing hole pulling the fish out of the water. Of course, when I was a boy I didn't get to do that very often, because my mom usually had some work for me to do around the house.

There was one time, though, when she said I could go and fish as long as I wanted. But she told me, "You'd better take along something to eat. You're going to get hungry if you plan on staying all day."

So I went into the kitchen to find something to take along for lunch. I didn't want to bother with making a sandwich—I was looking for something I could grab quick. I searched through the cupboards and found a brand new sack of pretzels. "That'll do," I thought. I grabbed my fishing gear and the sack of pretzels and headed for the pond.

My mom was right. I hadn't been fishing long enough to catch more than two or three fish when I started feeling hungry. So I opened the sack of pretzels and started munching.

Well, of course the pretzels made me thirsty and I began to wish I'd brought along something to drink. But I hadn't, so the only thing to do was to drink a little water from the pond. It was good clear spring water, so I knew it wouldn't do me any harm. Then, as I stooped over to get a sip from the pond, a question popped into my mind. I thought, "I wonder if fish like pretzels?"

I snapped a little piece off a pretzel and flipped it into the pond. *Blip!* A fish came up and swallowed the piece of pretzel. "That's great!" I said to myself. "They love pretzels!"

I tore open the pretzel sack and ground them up in my hands. Then I threw handful after handful of pretzel crumbs into the pond. The fish just made the water boil as they went after the pretzels, and

naturally the pretzels made the fish thirsty too. So they drank water from the pond, just like I did.

They ate pretzels and drank water, ate more pretzels and drank more water, and the pond was getting lower and lower all the time. I just sat back and watched with a big grin on my face. And it may be hard for you to believe, but the fish kept going until they drank up every drop of water in the pond. I just walked around and picked fish up off the bottom of the dry hole where the pond had once been.

So you can talk to me about your favorite fishing bait—worms or eggs or corn or whatever—but as far as I'm concerned, it's hard to find a better bait than pretzels. Unless maybe it's raisins.

You see, on another very similar occasion all I could find to make a quick lunch was a sack of raisins. I knew my mom would like the idea of my taking raisins along to eat because she always told me raisins were good for me. "They put iron in your blood," she'd say.

Once again I thought I'd see if fish had any taste for my food. I tossed a raisin into the pond. Sure enough—they liked raisins even better than pretzels.

All the while they were eating my raisins I was thinking, "Won't your mommas be proud of you for getting all that iron in your blood?" And then I got an idea. I reached into my back pocket and pulled out a magnet. I held it under the water, and the next thing I knew there was a fish stuck to it.

Yeah! Those fish had so much iron in their blood from eating my raisins I spent the rest of the afternoon pulling them out of the pond with a magnet! That was a little more interesting than just picking fish up from the dry ground, so I guess raisins are a little better bait than pretzels.

The Checker Playing
Hound Dog

When I was growing up, there was one man all the youngsters in our town admired. He was an old cowboy named Slim. He lived in a tumble-down shack on the other side of the tracks and every kid in town would go there to hear him tell about his experiences back in the days of open range cowboying. He'd talk about cattlemen and outlaws and horses he'd known.

Slim used to tell us, "Kids, the smartest thing on the range is a good cow pony. After that comes a sheep dog. And third in line is a man with a college education."

I wasn't so sure that was true, because Slim hadn't even finished the fourth grade, much less college, and he seemed to be the smartest man alive to me. But I had to agree that a dog can be smart. I had owned some pretty sharp ones myself. One of them was part retriever, and I think he was the smartest of them all.

Now, you may have seen dogs that can fetch back a stick you throw or play catch with a ball. Of course my dog could do all those things ever since he was a week old. But when this dog was full grown, he could understand anything I said to him and bring me whatever I asked for.

If I was playing down by the creek and got my feet wet, I'd tell my dog, "Go get me some dry socks." And in five minutes he'd be back with a pair of clean socks in his mouth.

Or if my friends and I decided to get up a ball game, I didn't have to run home and get my glove like the other kids. I'd just send my dog. Of course I'd have to tell him which one I wanted because I owned a fielder's glove and a catcher's mitt too. And he never once brought me the wrong one.

I was really proud of my dog and I thought he was just about the smartest dog there ever was, but I guess I found out different.

You see, one day I started bragging at school about my dog. I said I owned the smartest dog in town. A boy from across town said

he'd bet his dog was smarter than mine. We bet a dollar apiece—and that was a lot of money for a kid in those days—and we set the next Saturday as the day for the contest.

When Saturday arrived I took some of my friends and my dog and went to the vacant lot where we agreed to hold the contest. The kid from across town showed up with his friends and his dog, and we got started.

First we had our dogs do the regular tricks—sit, shake hands, roll over, stand up on their hind legs. My dog did those things easily. And he could also stand on just his two left legs or his right legs. He never got left and right confused either.

The kid from across town said that was nothing. He told his dog, "Go see if Mom's baking cookies." His dog ran off and came back in a few minutes. He nodded his head up and down. "Yep," the kid said, "my mom's baking cookies." And he told one of my friends to go see if it wasn't true. Sure enough, my friend came back and told us the kid's mother was baking chocolate chip cookies.

So I told my dog, "I'm hungry. Go get me an apple." He ran to my house and brought back a nice fat red apple in his jaws. He didn't poke any holes in it with his teeth either. "What do you say to that?" I asked the kid from across town.

"Nothin' much. Only watch this." Then he told his dog, "Go borrow Robert Sleaver's baseball." His dog ran down to Robert Sleaver's house and brought back the ball that was on the porch.

Now all the cross-town kids started saying that was the best trick of all. It's one thing for your dog to go to your own house and fetch something, they said, but it takes a really smart dog to know which one of your friend's houses you're talking about and go there to borrow something for you. They started hooting and laughing and said their friend had won the bet.

But I wasn't licked by a long shot. I pulled a dollar bill out of my pocket and held it out to my dog. I told him, "Run down to Franklin's store and get me a pack of Juicy Fruit gum."

My dog snapped the dollar out of my hand and was gone down the street. He came back in no time with a little brown paper sack in his mouth. I opened the sack and showed everyone what was inside—a pack of Juicy Fruit gum and ninety-five cents change. Now it was my friends' turn to laugh.

But the boy from across town said, "Wait a minute. How did your dog get the gum in the sack? And who gave him the change?"

I told him Mr. Franklin at the store knew my dog and would always put the gum and change in a sack for him to bring back to me.

"That's cheating!" the cross-town kids all shouted. "Your dog had help."

"But he picked out the right flavor of gum," I argued. "I'll bet your dog couldn't do that." My friends all agreed with me and a big argument began.

Well, there was only one thing to do. We'd have to talk to old cowboy Slim and let him settle the argument. So we all headed down to his shack across the railroad tracks. When we got there the door was standing open so we trooped right into the kitchen. Then we all burst out laughing.

There was Slim sitting at his kitchen table with a checker board in front of him. And sitting across the table was his big old flop-eared dog. And they were playing checkers!

Slim looked up from his game and gave us one of his slow, toothless grins. "What can I do for you kids?" he asked.

We all felt kind of foolish. "Well," we said, "we've been having a big argument about who owns the smartest dog in town. But you just settled it. Your dog is the smartest. He can play checkers!"

Slim kind of tipped his hat up and scratched his head with one finger. "Oh, he ain't so smart," he drawled. "I just beat him three games out of five."

That kind of taught me a lesson about bragging. Didn't teach me much about exaggerating though.

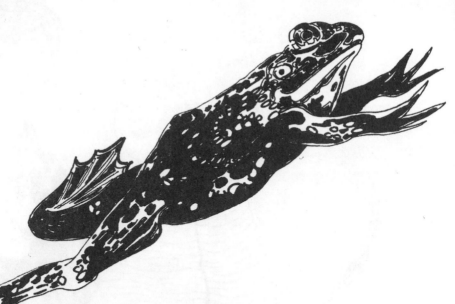

The Frog Leg Harvest

Whenever I had a little free time when I was a boy I'd head out to my favorite pond to catch a few fish or take a little swim. Or sometimes I'd catch frogs. It seemed like about a thousand bullfrogs used to sit on the bank of that pond and catch flies all day long. In the evening they'd just croak their heads off.

But if I wanted to catch any of those frogs, I'd have to sneak up very quietly. If they heard me coming, there'd be one big splash when all one thousand frogs hit the water at once.

One day in the fall of the year I asked my dad if I could go fishing after supper. "You'd better keep an eye on the weather," my dad warned. "It looks like there's a storm making over in the west." I looked up and saw there was some hard weather coming our way for sure. But I had no idea how suddenly it would arrive.

I set out across the fields with my fishing pole, whistling to myself and thinking about those big catfish waiting for my line. Over by the pond the frogs were holding a choir meeting—flapping their mouths like a nation of fools. Overhead I could see that the storm was easing in closer.

Well, it was fish I was after, not frogs, so I didn't care a hoot whether I scared the old croakers or not. I walked right up to the pond. I was about a fishing pole's length from the bank when the frogs took notice of me, and they all made a swan dive for the water.

Just about then the storm decided to swoop in. And the temperature dropped so fast the pond was already freezing by the time the frogs hit the water. And it froze up solid before their hind legs went under!

Imagine the sight I saw. There was the big glassy frozen pond before me—with two thousand little green frog legs sticking up like blades of grass.

Well that gave me an idea. I ran home and got the lawn mower. I mowed the frog legs down—*b-r-r-r-r-r-r-r!* I raked them up, packed them in ice, took them over to town and sold them to a high class restaurant. Yeah! Frog legs are really popular in those fancy restaurants. Rich folks pay a lot of money for them. I made out all right that time, didn't I?

And don't go feeling sorry for those frogs. They were all numb from the cold and didn't feel a thing. They stayed frozen in the pond all winter long under a thick layer of snow. And when the snow finally melted next spring, they sprouted the prettiest crop of new green legs —looked just like a field of winter wheat!

A Tall Christmas Tale

Several years ago I spent the first part of the winter in a cabin on Three Mile Mountain, which is just about the coldest spot south of north. In fact, the only thing to break the wind between the North Pole and the little pine tree that stood beside my cabin door was a two-strand barbed wire fence about 100 miles away. And that year one strand was down, so it was uncommonly cold.

But I was doing all right. I had plenty of warm clothes and lots of firewood. My cupboard was full of beans and biscuit flour. I had no reason to complain.

But when it got close to Christmas, I began to wish for something a little fancier to eat. I guess I was feeling a bit homesick and think-ing of all the fine meals I had eaten at the family table on Christmas. So the day before Christmas I decided to hunt me up a wild turkey to roast for Christmas dinner.

Early in the morning I built up the fire in my cabin so it would be nice and warm for me when I got back, and I set out with my shotgun. Golly, it was cold! The air kind of crackled around me as I walked through it—sort of like breaking through the thin skin of ice on a puddle. But I figured things had to warm up as the day went on.

I figured wrong. It got colder and colder, until finally I could scarcely break my way through the frozen air. If there were any turkeys in all that country, they weren't about to show their faces on such a cold day. So I decided to return to my cabin.

When I got back to the cabin, what do you suppose I saw? There, at the very top of the pine tree beside my cabin door perched a big fat gobbler! "Well," I said to myself, "I guess I believe in Santa Claus after all." I upped with my gun and cut loose.

There wasn't a sound! It was so cold, the report from my shot was frozen in the air before it reached my ears. And the buckshot only traveled about ten feet from the barrel of my gun before it lost traction in the icy air and came sliding back toward me. I ducked my head just in time, or I wouldn't be here to tell you about it. If my hat hadn't been frozen to my head, it would have been knocked off!

Well, I'd had enough of that cold. I decided to spend the rest of the day inside by the fire. I stomped into the cabin and pulled off my gloves and held my hands up close to the flames. I didn't feel a thing! But I knew my hands weren't frozen because I could bend the knuckles. Then I noticed the flames weren't moving. The fire in my fireplace was frozen solid! The flames just stood there like upside down icicles, giving off a pale orange glow.

I reached in and broke off a big flame—snap!—and held it in my hand. It didn't burn me at all. It was perfectly smooth and hard—and a little bit slippery. In fact, the flame slid right out of my hand and hit the big rock in front of the fireplace and shattered into a hundred pieces. Each little chip of flame was glowing orange or yellow or pale blue. You know what it reminded me of? Christmas lights! Yes, shiny Christmas lights that people in their comfortable homes in towns and cities all over the country had hanging on their Christmas trees.

I said to myself, "Maybe I can't have turkey for Christmas dinner. And maybe I can't be warm and comfortable. But by golly, I'm going to have a Christmas tree!" I tied a short piece of string to each chip of fire that lay there on the hearth rock. Then I went outside and hung them all over the pine tree by the cabin door, from the bottom limbs as high up as I could reach.

That made me feel some better. I went back inside and piled every blanket I could find on the bed and climbed in. I figured I'd just stay there under the covers until the weather warmed up a bit.

I must have been worn out by all that cold because I fell asleep and slept the whole day away, and the night too. I didn't wake up until the next morning when I heard a shotgun go off—*bang!* I dived under the bed wondering who was after me, and for what. Then as my senses came back to me I understood what had happened. The cold had let up some and the air was warm enough for the sound of my shot from the day before to thaw out.

I pulled myself from under the bed and walked to the door. When I opened it, I was struck by a blast of heat. My frozen fire had thawed out too, and set the pine tree ablaze. It's a pure wonder the whole cabin didn't go up in flames with it.

I was just turning away from the door, feeling about as foolish as a man who looks into a gas tank with a lighted match, when I noticed a delicious smell. I looked up, and sure enough, the fire had cooked the turkey in the top of the tree—roasted it to a turn!

I got me a long pole and knocked the turkey from the tree and got things ready for a Christmas feast. But, you know, that poor bird was so starved that the more of it I ate, the hungrier I got. I must have downed ten pounds of turkey, until I felt so hollow my stomach thought my throat had been cut.

Well, that was the last straw. I whipped up a quick batch of biscuits and ate my fill. Then I packed my gear and left that place, swearing a petrified oath to myself that I'd spend the rest of my Christmases at home where I belong.

A Stack of Fog

One summer my friend and I worked together on a farm. We slept in a shed behind the farm house and we got up every morning when the first rooster crowed at about four o'clock. We worked in all kinds of weather. If there was a job that needed to be done we did it, no matter what tricks nature was up to outside.

One morning the rooster's crow woke us up as usual and we were dressed and ready to get to work by first light. But no light came. I looked outside and saw why. Fog lay so thick around the farm that the daylight couldn't get through.

But the farmer had told us to put new shingles on the barn roof that day and, fog or no fog, the job had to be done. So we dressed good and warm and started out the door. But we bounced right back inside. The fog was so thick we couldn't walk through it. It was just like a big wet sponge. You could push your arm into it, even part it with your two hands, but as soon as you let go, it sprang right back into place.

When I saw that, I told my friend we'd have to take it in turns. I'd hold the fog open till he took a step. Then he'd hold it for me. By leap-frogging that way, we finally reached the barn.

We made our way up the ladder and started nailing new shingles on the roof. Once we got into the rhythm of the work, we didn't let up for a minute, and those shingles went on at a furious pace. We hardly noticed that any time had passed when the farmer's wife rang the bell for lunch.

Well, we groped around until we located the ladder and then climbed down and team-worked our way back to the house to eat. While we were eating the sun started burning through the fog and, by the time we'd finished, the sky was clear. We figured we'd better get back to work. But when we stepped outside, my friend pointed toward the barn and howled with laughter.

Do you know what we had done? We had been so caught up in our work we hadn't noticed that we'd reached the edge of the roof and we'd nailed shingles right out onto that thick fog for about ten feet beyond the roof. What a sight that was! A big pile of fog, like a gray hay stack, was held in place beside the barn by the shingles we'd nailed onto it.

"Should we pull up those shingles and let the fog loose?" we asked the farmer.

"No," he said. "We'll just leave them there. A shedful of fog might come in handy."

And it did. The farmer's kids loved to play hide-and-seek in it. His wife gathered a barrelful and kept it in the kitchen to add to biscuit batter. Those biscuits were so light they'd practically float up off your plate into your mouth. And when the stack was nearly gone, they dried out the rest of it and used it to fill pillows and mattresses. It made wonderful stuffing—even fluffier than feathers.

The Water Silo

When I was a boy, I'd sometimes spend the summer on my uncle's farm. They didn't have running water on that farm—just a stone well in the yard—and whenever I stayed there it was my job to draw water from the well. I guess I must have pulled a thousand miles of well rope every summer. But then I got some help in a way I never would have expected.

One afternoon, we saw the telltale black funnel of a tornado coming toward us across the prairie. My aunt and uncle shooed all the kids into the storm cellar where we'd be safe, and we waited out the storm. From the ruckus outside, you'd think the world was coming apart at the seams.

Then, when things quieted down, we went back outside. The house and barn were still standing, but we could see from all the furniture, telephone poles, haystacks and whatnot lying around that the twister had passed right through the yard. The kerosene can that always sat on the back porch had been turned inside out, with the shiny

metal showing outside and the bright red paint turned in. Luckily none of the kerosene had spilled, though.

We all gazed around in amazement, but my uncle was the most puzzled of all. He kept scratching his head and staring at the barn. "There's something different about that barn," he said. "But danged if I can see what it is." We kids and Auntie agreed that something had changed, but we couldn't figure it out either. We all gawked for a while longer. Then Auntie put a stop to it.

"I can't stand here gaping all day," she said. "I've got dinner to fix. And you kids have chores to get done." She handed me the pail. "Go fetch me some water from the well."

I ran off, but was back in a minute with an empty pail. "Where's the water?" Auntie asked.

"Where's the well, you mean," I said. "Auntie, the well's gone. I can't find it anywhere."

"The well's gone?" she said. "Whoever heard of such a thing!"

She went striding out to where the well had been, and, sure enough, there wasn't a trace of it. She looked all around in confusion. Then she laughed. "Why, sure," she said. "That's what looks different about the barn. There's a stone silo standing beside it. That was never there before. Don't you see what happened? The twister pulled up our well and stood it over there beside the barn. Run and tell your uncle."

I did. And the first thing he did was to put a spigot on the bottom of the well. I never had to pull a well rope again. I'd just run over to that stone silo and drain off a pail of water whenever we needed some.

Hard Boiled Eggs

In the summer, one of the familiar sights in these parts is a lizard carrying a stick in its mouth. That way, if it gets tired out running from one shady bush to another and has to stop and rest, it can climb onto the stick to keep its feet and tail from being scorched by the hot sand. That's on cool days, of course. When it's really hot they don't come out at all.

Well, one summer I decided to go out to the country and spend a couple of weeks on my uncle's farm. My mom drove me out there one morning, and I knew it was a really hot day because on the way out from town we saw a coyote chasing a jackrabbit. And they were both walking.

My mom dropped me off at the farm about midday, and things sure didn't get any more comfortable as the day wore on. Finally we had to build a fire in the stove to cool the house down.

The heat didn't bother my uncle any, though. He went right on doing the chores around the farm. When he came back from the hen house with a basket of eggs, I told him, "Uncle, I'm about to die from this heat."

"Yes," he replied, "it is kind of a warm spell we're having."

"Warm spell!" I said. "Why, I'll bet this is the hottest it's ever been!"

"Maybe you're right," my uncle nodded. "Let's just see." He took one of the eggs from the basket and cracked it open. "Nope," he said. "It was hotter last week. This egg is still a little soft. Last week my hens were laying them plumb hard boiled!"

Trick Lightning

It's been many years since I've seen lightning like we had when I was a boy. Every afternoon in summer a thunder storm would bombard the countryside. And then, along about dark, when the storm was kind of resting and catching its breath, we'd sit on the front porch and watch the lightning flashes broad jump from one horizon to the other.

Sometimes the lightning would make the sky bright for so long the birds would wake up and start singing. And one time an especially long-winded lightning bolt made it look like midday for about five minutes.

Over in town an old dog that was sleeping in an alley woke up and thought it was time for breakfast. He started ambling across the street toward the butcher shop to beg for some scraps of meat. Suddenly, the lightning went out and the thunder started roaring.

That foolish old mutt heard the noise and thought he was being run over by a semi truck. He lay down in the street and took himself for dead.

The next morning he was still there blocking traffic, and no one could convince him to move. He was smart enough to know that dead dogs don't get up and walk away. Finally the butcher got an idea. He brought out a whole sack of soup bones and spread them all around that old hound. The dog opened one eye and saw that he was surrounded by bones, and he thought sure he had died and gone to heaven. He jumped up and started romping around like a young pup.

You can imagine how the whole town got a good laugh out of that. But that old flea bag wasn't as dumb as everyone thought. From that day on, whenever he got really hungry, he'd go right back out to the middle of the street and drop dead again!

High Wind

One thing we could always depend on around here when I was growing up was the wind. Sometimes a stranger would ask us, "Does the wind always blow like this?"

We'd answer, "No sir, sometimes it blows harder." And that was no joke. The buildings never had weather vanes or wind socks on them, the way they do in other places. If you wanted to know which way the wind was blowing, all you had to do was look out the window and see which way the buildings were leaning.

But I remember one time when we had an especially windy weekend. The wind blew all the feathers off our chickens. And their eggs came out scrambled for the next couple of days. One poor woman was caught out in that wind and it blew her up against a wall—knocked her so flat she could eat nothing but buttered tortillas and thin slices of cheese. It was a real howler, I'll tell you.

One Monday morning when I was riding the bus to school I looked out at the barbed wire fence alongside the road and saw that all the barbs had been blown down to the southeast corner of each section. And when I got to school, I found out my best friend was absent that day. I was worried about him. I was afraid maybe he'd been blown away over the weekend.

I fretted about my friend all day, and when the bell finally rang for the end of school, I ran out to his house to see if he was all right. He lived way out at the very edge of town.

I arrived at my friend's house all out of breath and asked his mother if anything was wrong with him. "No, he's just fine," she told me. "He'll be home when the school bus gets here—in about thirty minutes."

"When the bus gets here? What do you mean?" I asked. "The buses left school a long time ago. And besides, he doesn't ride a bus to school. And on top of that, he wasn't in school today anyway."

Then his mother explained, "He couldn't go to your school today. You see, that wind we had over the weekend was so strong it blew the city limit to the other side of our house. We lived in your school district last week, but this week we're in the Carlton school district."

"Carlton," I said. "Why, that's twenty-five miles away!"

"That's why it will take another thirty minutes for him to get home," my friend's mother told me.

And there was nothing we could do about it. My friend had to ride the bus to school in the next town for almost a month until the survey crew finally got out there and put the city limit back where it had been before the wind moved it.

My Alarm Clock

One year I thought I'd spend the whole summer out in the mountains hunting. The first thing I needed to do was find a good place for my base camp.

Well, I was going up the side of a mountain looking for a good campsite and I came to a nice smooth ledge—looked like the perfect place to set up my base. Then I looked out across the canyon and I saw there was a high cliff straight across from my camp. I thought, "I'll bet there's a good echo here." So I turned toward the cliff and hollered, "Helloooo...."

I waited, but no echo came back. "I guess I was wrong about that," I said to myself and went on laying out my camp. Then I went off to hunt for the day.

In the evening I came back and built a fire. I had cooked my supper and was just sitting down to eat, when I heard a voice call, "Helloooo...."

Why, it had taken all day for my voice to get over to the cliff and for the echo to get back!

Now, that gave me an idea. That night when I was ready to sleep, I laid out my bedroll and banked the fire good. Then I turned toward the cliff and hollered, "Wake up you foool...."

I went to sleep—slept like a baby—and just about sunrise a voice called to me, "Wake up you foool...." It worked perfectly. In fact, I used that echo for an alarm clock all summer long.

Well, you know, it was lonesome out there in the mountains all by myself, and that echo was the only companion I had. Sometimes I'd get up in the morning and call across the canyon, "How ya doinnn'...?"

I'd go off and hunt for the day and come back in the evening, and the echo would greet me, "Pretty good. How're yooouuuu....?"

The Lodgepole Toothpick

When I was a young man, I lived way high up in the Rocky Mountains. There was a tall snow-covered range on either side of the valley I lived in. To the east was the Stoney Ridge range and to the west the Salt River Mountains. The Salt River itself was a little stream that wound its way through the valley.

I lived in a cabin a short way up on the slope of the Salt River range. And the second winter I spent in that cabin, a terrible blizzard blew in one night.

I woke up in the morning and looked at the window of my cabin and it was pure white. So I knew the snow was pretty deep. I went over to the door and threw my shoulder against it, but it didn't budge —not half an inch.

Well, I had a pretty good supply of food and firewood. I wasn't worried. But several days later I had to tear up some floor boards in the cabin for stove wood. And I had about a handful of flour left in the cupboard to make a hotcake for breakfast. I knew I had to get out of that cabin and get some food and firewood. The only way I could see to do it was to take down the stovepipe and climb out onto the roof.

That's what I did. I let the fire burn down in the stove. Then I took down the pipe. I put my axe out onto the roof and hoisted myself out after it. When I got out onto the roof, I saw that the snow towered about thirty feet above the roof of my cabin. The heat from the stove had kept it melted directly above, or I'd really have been trapped.

Well, I got busy with my axe chopping footholds, and I climbed up to the top of the snow. I looked around, and in every direction I saw solid white. The snow was up over the tops of the tallest trees! I didn't know what to do.

Then I looked around again, and over in the Stoney Ridge range, at the top of a cliff, there was a big lodgepole pine tree kind of growing out at an angle, so it wasn't covered with snow. Well, that looked like my only chance to find some firewood, so I headed in that direction.

But as I got closer to the tree, it began to look like a big pile of fur and feathers. I couldn't figure that out. Then it began to make sense. Of course, as the snow got deep and covered up a tree, all the animals and birds living in the tree would have to move on to another. But that tree would get covered too, so they'd have to keep moving. Finally all the critters for miles around wound up in the one tree that wasn't buried in snow. I had located meat and firewood in the same place!

When I got to the tree I found that all the animals had frozen to death, so I just went to picking and choosing like a person at the meat counter in a supermarket. I tossed the animals off to the side and cut a strip of bark from the tree to tie them together with. Then I went to work chopping down the tree.

Now, it was a big fat lodgepole pine tree, so it took me quite a while to chop it down. Then I started cleaning off the branches and cutting them into stove lengths.

Well, there I was with my axe, chopping on the last branch of the tree, when all of a sudden that big fat lodgepole pine log spun around and went sliding down the mountainside. I saw it hit the bottom of the valley, cross the Salt River and start up the other side.

I thought it would jump over the ridge and head on into the next valley. But, no, it just reached the top of the ridge and back it came toward me. Well, I was ready for it. I was going to catch it with my axe as it came by. But the log was traveling a lot faster than I figured. I missed it by about six inches, and back the other way it slid—just kicking up a rooster-tail of snow behind it.

I thought, "I'm not going to risk my life trying to catch that log. It must be going ninety miles an hour." Besides, I already had a good supply of firewood. So I just gathered up my things and went back to the cabin. I climbed in through the roof, set the stovepipe back in place, built up a fire, and I was right back in business.

But even all that food and firewood couldn't last forever. One morning I had to knock the shelves out of the cupboard for firewood, and I was frying up the last old fat squirrel I had for breakfast, when I heard a trickling sound over by the window.

I looked over there and saw the tiniest sliver of light coming in the top of the window. So after I ate my breakfast I went to the door and laid my shoulder into it. It opened about two inches. I hit it again and it opened a little wider. It took me five, six, maybe seven tries to get the door open wide enough to get out.

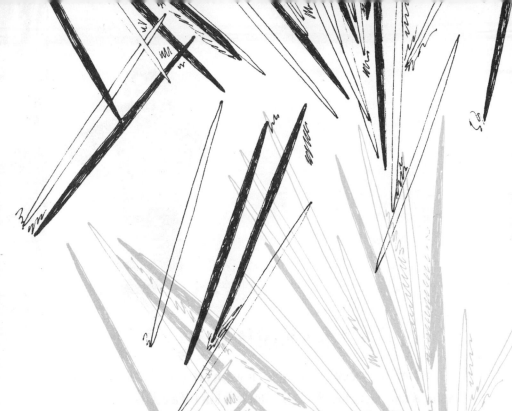

The first thing I thought of was to get down to the closest town and get some food and firewood. I started off in that direction and I came to a big gully in the snow. It was where my log had been sliding back and forth. Well, I had to get to the bottom of that valley anyway, since that was where the town was, so I decided to walk on down the gully. Besides, I was curious to know what had happened to my pine log.

I got to the bottom of the valley, and there was my log, still sliding back and forth—going about three inches at a time. And do you know what? With all that seesawing back and forth that big old lodgepole pine log had worn itself down to the size of a toothpick!

Yes, sir! I picked it up and put it in my pocket and I have kept it ever since. Come see me some day and I'll show it to you.

The Split Dog

When I was a boy, I had a dog. He wasn't very big. In fact, he only stood about a foot tall. And his color was kind of a yellowish brown.

My friends would all make fun of my dog. They would tell me, "Your dog looks like a rat! Look at that long skinny tail he's got."

Well, those boys all had big dogs like German shepherds their dads had paid a lot of money for. But I'll tell you one thing—my dog could run faster than any of their big dogs. And he could catch rabbits too. He could catch rabbits like no dog you ever saw. That dog just loved to chase rabbits.

Well, one day we were walking in a field together—my dog and I—and a rabbit jumped up and took off across the field. My little dog was right behind him. They were dodging back and forth, racing through the tall grass.

Then they came to the corner of the field, where there was a big telephone pole. And there was one of these guy wires coming down at an angle to help hold up the pole. Well, the rabbit went zinging right by the wire, and my little dog was right behind him. But my dog didn't see the wire. He ran smack into it. And it split him in two—from the tip of his nose to the tip of his tail. He just flopped over in two pieces.

I went running up there and grabbed those two pieces and slapped my dog back together again. I tore off my shirt and wrapped it around him. I carried him back home in my arms. Tears were coming out of my eyes. Why, that dog was like a member of our family. We loved that little dog. And I thought for sure he was a goner!

But when I got him home, there was still a little twinkle in his eye. That little dog was still alive! So I made him a nice soft bed. I put it in the kitchen next to the stove where it was always nice and warm. I poured medicine all over the shirt, so he wouldn't get infected. If it was a nice day, I'd carry him outside and put him in the sunshine, because the sun would help to heal him.

I took good care of my little dog, and about a month later, I could see that it had paid off. His little tail started to wag. And about two months later, I was eating my breakfast one morning, and I heard my little dog bark. I was so excited! I thought, "If he's well enough to bark, he must be just about all healed up."

So I picked him up and carried him out to the front yard. I laid him down on the grass and started to unwrap the shirt from around him. When I got the shirt off, you know what I found? Well, I had been so worried, and in such a big hurry, when I put my dog back together—I had put him together wrong way around! Two legs were sticking down—but the other two legs were sticking up!

I thought, "Oh, no! I ruined my little dog." But I couldn't have been more wrong. If he was a good dog before, he was twice as good now. He'd run on two legs till they got tired, then he'd flop over and run on the other two legs!

That little dog could run coming and going all day along. And he could bark at both ends!

The Gum Chewing Rattler

When I was a kid, I had a bad habit—I just loved to chew bubblegum. I always had a juicy wad of bubblegum in my mouth—two or three pieces at the same time—just chomping away.

My teacher would see the wad in my mouth and snap, "Get rid of that gum!" I would have to take the gum out of my mouth and wrap it up in some paper and throw it in the waste basket. But I didn't really care because I always kept another package of bubblegum right in my shirt pocket.

But my mom was the one who would really get mad at me, because I would forget to take the gum out of my pocket and throw my shirt in the wash. It would come out of the washing machine with a big, gunky stain around the pocket. My mom would say, "Look at this! You've ruined another shirt!" But then one day something happened that changed her mind and she never got mad at me again for carrying gum in my shirt pocket.

One day I was walking around out in the desert, kind of day

dreaming—chomping on my bubblegum and not paying attention to where I was going. And I stepped right on a rattlesnake's tail!

Well, the snake couldn't rattle and warn me because I was standing on his tail. So he didn't even worry about warning me. He just came striking up through the air, aiming his fangs right at my heart. He hit me—*bam!*—right on the shirt pocket. And that's where I was carrying my spare bubblegum. The rattlesnake's fangs stuck in the bubblegum!

There I stood with my foot on a rattlesnake's tail—and with his fangs stuck in my shirt pocket. He was thrashing around and whipping up against me, and I was so scared I couldn't move. I just stood there, staring into his beady little eyes. Those eyes were just looking hate at me! And he was working his jaws, trying to get his fangs out of the gum so that he could get back at me and bite me good!

But, of course, as he was working his jaws to get his fangs out of the bubblegum, the gum kept getting softer and softer. And the next thing I knew there was a little pink bubble coming up out of his mouth! It got bigger and bigger till it was the size of a basketball!

I got up all my courage. I brought my hand up slowly and—*pop!* —I burst the bubble! The snake went flying back and his head hit on a rock. It killed him.

But that did take all my courage. I fainted and fell out in the other direction. I didn't come home for lunch and my mom came looking for me. She found me lying on the ground fainted out cold. And lying in the other direction was the dead rattlesnake.

She asked me what had happened, and I told her the same story I just told. You know what? She didn't believe it either.

Fur-Bearing Fish

When I was a boy, my best friend was sort of a scientist, and he almost made some important discoveries. For example, he had a hamster once and he decided to see if he could train it to live without eating. What he did was so simple I'm surprised no one ever thought of it before. He just gave the hamster a little less food each day. He just about had the little critter trained where it could live on nothing but fresh air and sunshine when it died on him. I tried to talk him into trying again, but he never liked to repeat an experiment.

Then there was the time he got a chemistry set for his birthday. He brought it over to my house to show me, and my dad asked him, "What are you going to invent with that chemistry set—anything useful?"

My friend looked at my dad and thought for a minute, then said, "I think I'll invent a tonic to grow hair on a bald head." Well, my dad's head was pretty bald, so he laughed at my friend's remark. He thought it was a good joke.

But my friend wasn't kidding. He went to work that very day trying out different combinations of chemicals to see if any would grow hair.

For several weeks he worked on his experiment, off and on. Then one rainy day he called me up and said he was sure he had the right combination. He said he had a tonic that would grow hair on any human or animal that used it. I told him to bring his hair tonic over to my house so I could see it.

Well, there was an arroyo between our two houses. Usually it was just a dry sandy wash, but that day the rain had turned it into a regular river. My friend came running through the rain toward my house, holding the bottle of hair tonic up high in his right hand, and when he reached the bank of the arroyo he jumped.

Durned if he didn't lose his footing and slip. He landed a little past the middle of the stream. Luckily the current wasn't too swift and he was able to slog on across. But when he slipped, he dropped the bottle of hair tonic into the stream.

The current carried it away and surely dashed the bottle against a rock somewhere downstream. There went the result of all my friend's hard work. And he hadn't written down the formula, so he'd have to start all over again. But I told you how my friend felt about repeating an experiment. So that was the end of that. At least we thought so.

A few weeks later we went fishing at the river that was about two miles from where we lived. The easiest way to get to the river was to just walk on down the arroyo that ran between our houses, so we did that. We started fishing close to where the arroyo emptied into the river.

The first fish we caught gave us quite a surprise. It was covered with fur. "Who ever heard of a fur-bearing fish" my friend said.

Then we both realized what had happened. His hair-growing tonic had been carried down to the river by the arroyo, so naturally all the fish living close to the mouth of the arroyo had grown hair!

Some of the ones we caught were really shaggy. "In another week's time these fish are going to need a haircut bad!" I joked to my friend.

But he didn't take it as a joke. He started thinking about what I said and it gave him an idea. A week later he showed up at my house wearing a white shirt with the tails untucked. In one hand he had a fence post painted with red, white and blue stripes spiraling around it—sort of like the old-time barber poles. In the other hand he had a pair of scissors. "Let's go fishing," he said.

Well, that was the strangest fishing gear I'd ever seen, but I tagged along just to see what he had in mind. We walked down the arroyo to the river and set the pole up on the bank. Then he started clicking his scissors and calling out, "Haircuts, seventy-five cents. Step right up!"

And durned if those bushy-haired fish didn't start lining up for a trim! As quick as they'd come up out of the water I'd grab them and pop them into my creel. And my friend kept calling out, "Next! Next!" until every last one of the fur-bearing fish was caught.

So now that really was the end of it. But, you know, I wish we'd left a few of those hairy fish in the river, because I've always wondered if their babies would have had fur too. I guess I'll never know.

The Inside Out Coyote

Sometimes I like to get in my truck and just drive up into the mountains. I'll follow any old road just to find where it goes and see what I can see. I remember one day when I drove up a bumpy dirt road for about ten miles. It took me into a pretty little canyon. Then all of a sudden the road stopped. I got out to look around and found a trail on up the canyon started just where the road ended.

Well, I was sort of stiff from lurching over the bumps in my truck and I thought a short hike up the trail would be just the thing I needed to stretch out the kinks in my back before I started driving back down the road. So I headed up the trail.

The sides of the canyon were really steep and the trail up it rose at a pretty sharp angle too. I followed the trail for about half a mile, and then it ended against a sheer cliff.

Well, I was in no mood to scale a cliff, so I turned to go back to my truck. Just when I turned, I saw a coyote on the trail below me, maybe a hundred yards away and headed in my direction.

At first I was happy. I'm always glad to run into wildlife when I'm out in the mountains. But then I got worried. The coyote was behaving very strangely—sort of weaving and staggering as he came up the trail.

I thought, "Oh, no! Don't tell me I've run into a rabid coyote." I had heard stories of people meeting up with mad dogs or wild animals with rabies, but I never thought it could happen to me.

But as the coyote got closer I could see he was foaming at the mouth and his shoulders were all flecked with foam. It sure looked like I was up against a mad coyote. And of all places for it to happen! There I was with a cliff behind me and the walls of the canyon beside me so steep I could never outrun a coyote going up them. I didn't know what to do.

My mind was racing a mile a minute, and the only idea it came up with was to startle the coyote somehow so that I could get around him. Maybe I could outrun him going downhill. But the coyote was getting closer all the time and I hadn't figured out a way to scare him.

Finally, when he was only a few yards away, I decided I'd hit him on the nose with my fist. That would hurt. And before he could react, I'd jump over him and run.

The coyote was just a few paces away from me when he noticed I was there. He started growling and chomping his jaws and the foam really flowed from his mouth.

He charged toward me and I swung my fist as hard as I could, aiming right for the tip of his nose. But just when I swung, the coyote opened his jaws wide and my fist went into his mouth. Well, I had already committed myself, and the only thing to do was to follow through. I drove my fist right down the coyote's throat and deep into his body. Finally I felt a little nub—sort of like a button—far down inside his body. I knew it had to be the base of his tail.

I held that nub tight between my thumb and forefinger and jerked. And the coyote just turned inside out like a glove! He staggered off down the trail in the other direction. Why, he never even knew what hit him.

THE ILLUSTRATOR

Lucy Jelinek is an artist-designer who has worked in New Mexico since 1978. Santa Fe Pre-Print, Ms. Jelinek's company, is a graphic design firm specializing in publications. She has designed and illustrated eight books by Joe Hayes.

THE PUBLISHER

Mariposa Printing & Publishing was established in 1980. Our goal is to provide quality commercial printing to the Santa Fe community and to provide quality-crafted, limited edition publications in various literary fields.

Your comments and suggestions are appreciated. Contact Joe Mowrey, owner-production manager, Mariposa Printing & Publishing, 922 Baca Street, Santa Fe, New Mexico (505) 988-5582.